The Room on the Broom Play

Written by
Julia Donaldson

Illustrated by
Axel Scheffler

First published 2018 by Macmillan Children's Books
an imprint of Pan Macmillan
20 New Wharf Road, London N1 9RR
Associated companies throughout the world
www.panmacmillan.com
www.roomonthebroom.com

ISBN 978-1-5098-8263-2

Based on the bestselling picture book *Room on the Broom*
by Julia Donaldson and Axel Scheffler

1 3 5 7 9 8 6 4 2

A CIP catalogue record for this book is available from the British Library.

Printed in Spain

Contents

A Letter from Julia Donaldson

When I was little, my sister and I liked to create imaginary characters and put on shows. And when I was a teenager, I wanted to be an actress. Instead I became an author and wrote lots of books, but I've always loved the theatre, and writing and acting in plays too.

When I was Children's Laureate, one of my projects was to encourage children, parents and teachers to enjoy acting out stories. I often go on school visits and put on events at festivals and theatres. I like to invite children onto the stage to take part in the show.

In this play book you'll find a script which you can use to put on your very own performance of *Room on the Broom*. There are fun ideas for putting on your play, as well as music and words from the *Room on the Broom* song to add to your performance.

But now the lights are going down, the curtain is up and it's time for the show! I hope you have a wonderful time.

Julia Donaldson

The Room on the Broom Play

The Characters

Narrator 1

Narrator 2

Narrator 3

Narrator 4

Narrator 5

Narrator 6

Witch

Cat

Dog

Bird

Frog

Dragon

Wind

You can easily vary the number of narrators.
 See page 26 for ideas on performing the play
with groups of different sizes.

Narrator stands to the side of the stage as the curtain opens. Enter Witch and Cat on a broomstick, swaying as if flying in the wind. Witch has a cauldron and a wand.

 The witch had a cat and a very tall hat,
And long ginger hair which she wore in a plait.
How the cat purred

Cat purrs.

6

And how the witch grinned,

Witch grins at the audience.

 As they sat on their broomstick
and flew through the wind.
But how the witch wailed

Witch wails.

 and how the cat spat,

Cat spits.

 When the wind blew so wildly it blew off the hat.

Enter Wind, blowing at Witch's hat. Wind takes the hat from Witch's head and throws it offstage. Exit Wind.

 Down!

 cried the witch, and they flew to the ground.
They searched for the hat
but no hat could be found.

Witch and Cat climb off the broomstick and look around the stage.

 Then out of the bushes
on thundering paws
There bounded a dog
with the hat in his jaws.

Enter Dog with the hat in its mouth.
Dog drops the hat at Witch's feet.
She picks it up and puts it on.

 He dropped it politely,
then eagerly said,
As the witch pulled the hat
firmly down on her head,

 I am a dog, as keen as can be.
Is there room on the broom
for a dog like me?

 Yes!

 cried the witch, and the dog
clambered on.

Witch, Cat and Dog climb on
the broomstick.

 The witch tapped the broomstick
and whoosh! they were gone.

Witch taps the broomstick with her wand. Witch, Cat and Dog sway as if flying in the wind.

Exit Narrator 1. Enter Narrator 2.

 Over the fields and the forests they flew.
The dog wagged his tail and the stormy wind blew.
The witch laughed aloud and held on to her hat,
But away blew the bow from her long ginger plait!

Witch laughs and clutches her hat. Enter Wind, blowing at the bow on Witch's plait. Wind pulls off the bow and throws it offstage. Exit Wind.

Down!

 cried the witch, and they flew to the ground.
They searched for the bow
but no bow could be found.

Witch and Cat climb off the broomstick and look around the stage.

 Then out from a tree, with an earsplitting shriek,
There flapped a green bird with the bow in her beak.

Enter Bird, shrieking and flapping, with the bow in her mouth.
Bird drops the bow at Witch's feet. Witch picks it up.

 She dropped it politely and bent her head low,
Then said as the witch tied her plait in a bow,

Witch fixes the bow back onto her plait.

 I am a bird, as green as can be.
Is there room on the broom for a bird like me?

Yes!

 cried the witch, so the bird fluttered on.
The witch tapped the broomstick
and whoosh! they were gone.

Witch, Cat, Dog and Bird all climb onto the broomstick.
Witch taps the broomstick and then they all sway as if
flying in the wind.

Exit Narrator 2. Enter Narrator 3.

 Over the reeds and the rivers they flew.
The bird shrieked with glee
and the stormy wind blew.

Bird shrieks. Enter Wind blowing.

 They shot through the sky to the back of beyond.
The witch clutched her bow
but let go of her wand.

Wind blows at the wand. Witch drops it and Wind throws it offstage. Exit Wind.

 Down!

cried the witch, and they flew to the ground.
They searched for the wand
but no wand could be found.

*Witch, Cat, Dog and Bird climb off the broomstick and
look around the stage.*

Then all of a sudden from out of a pond
Leapt a dripping wet frog with a dripping wet wand.

*Enter Frog, hopping and carrying the wand. Frog drops the
wand at Witch's feet.*

He dropped it politely, then said with a croak
As the witch dried the wand on a fold of her cloak,

Witch wipes the wand on her cloak.

I am a frog, as clean as can be.
Is there room on the broom for a frog like me?

Yes!

 said the witch, so the frog bounded on.
The witch tapped the broomstick
and whoosh! they were gone.

*Witch, Cat, Dog, Bird and Frog
climb onto the broomstick. Witch
taps her broomstick, and they all
sway as if flying in the wind.*

Exit Narrator 3. Enter Narrator 4.

 Over the moors
and the mountains they flew.
The frog jumped for joy . . .

*Frog does a big jump. The broom
breaks, with Witch on the front
and the animals at the back. The
animals let go of the broom and
fall over.*

 . . . and the broom snapped
in two! Down fell the cat
and the dog and the frog.
Down they went tumbling
into a bog.

The animals crawl offstage where they get under a brown sheet.

The witch's half-broomstick flew into a cloud,
And the witch heard a roar that was scary and loud . . .

Dragon roars from offstage and then enters.

I am a dragon, as mean as can be,
And I'm planning to have WITCH AND CHIPS for my tea!

No!

cried the witch, flying higher and higher.
The dragon flew after her, breathing out fire.

*Witch flies her broken broomstick around the stage or
into the audience, chased by Dragon.*

Help!

cried the witch, flying down to the ground.
She looked all around but no help could be found.

*Witch climbs off her broken broomstick and looks around
for help.*

The dragon drew nearer and, licking his lips,
Said,

(licking his lips) Maybe this once I'll have witch
without chips.

Dragon seizes Witch and looks as if he's about to eat her.

Exit Narrator 4. Enter Narrator 5.

 But just as he planned
to begin on his feast,
From out of a ditch
rose a horrible beast.

*The animals enter under the sheet
and advance towards Dragon.*

 It was tall, dark and sticky,
and feathered and furred.
It had four frightful heads,
it had wings like a bird.
And its terrible voice,
when it started to speak,
Was a yowl

 Miaow!

 and a growl

 Grrr!

 and a croak

 Ribbit!

 and a shriek.

 Aaaagh!

 Miaow! Grrr! Ribbit! Aaaagh!

 It dripped and it squelched as it strode from the ditch,
And it said to the dragon,

 Buzz off! –
THAT'S MY WITCH!

 The dragon drew back and he started to shake.

Frightened Dragon shakes and moves away from the animals.

 I'm sorry!

 he spluttered.

 I made a mistake.
It's nice to have met you,
but now I must fly.

 And he spread out his
wings and was off
through the sky.

*Exit Dragon,
flapping wings.*

Narrator 5 exits, removing the brown sheet from the animals on the way. Enter Narrator 6.

 Then down flew the bird
and down jumped the frog.

Bird and Frog jump down and cuddle up to the witch.

 Down climbed the cat, and

Cat cuddles up to the witch too. Dog wipes his brow and joins the rest of the group.

 Phew!

 said the dog. And,

 Thank you, oh, thank you!

 the grateful witch cried.

 Without you I'd be in that dragon's inside.

 Then she filled up her cauldron
and said with a grin,

Witch picks up her cauldron and holds it out.

 Find something, everyone, throw something in!

Animals search for things to throw in the cauldron.

 So the frog found a lily,
the cat found a cone,
The bird found a twig,
and the dog found a bone.

Animals throw their objects into the cauldron. Witch stirs the cauldron with her wand.

They threw them all in and the witch stirred them well,
And while she was stirring, she muttered a spell.

 Iggety, ziggety, zaggety, ZOOM!

Stagehands bring three chairs and a tall stool onstage and set them up one behind the other.

 Then out rose . . .
. . . A TRULY MAGNIFICENT BROOM!
With seats for the witch and the cat and the dog,
A nest for the bird and a shower for the frog.

Yes!

cried the witch, and they all clambered on.

Cat, Dog and Witch take their seats on the chairs. Bird sits on the stool and Frog stands behind Bird. Narrator holds up Frog's hand above his head to look like a shower attachment.

 The witch tapped the broomstick and whoosh! they were gone.

Witch taps the new broomstick and they all sway as if flying. Lights dim.

The Room on the Broom Song

I am a cat, as lean as can be. Is there
I am a dog, as keen as can be. Is there
I am a bird, as green as can be. Is there
I am a frog, as clean as can be. Is there

room on the broom for a cat like me? Yes, yes, yes!
room on the broom for a dog like me? Yes, yes, yes!
room on the broom for a bird like me? Yes, yes, yes!
room on the broom for a frog like me? Yes, yes . . . no!

I am a dra – gon, as mean as can be. Is there

room on the broom for a dra–gon like me? No, no, no!

Off you go! Ho – ho – ho ho – ho – ho HO!

I am a cat, as LEAN as can be.
Is there room on the broom for a cat like me?
Yes, yes, yes!

I am a dog, as KEEN as can be.
Is there room on the broom for a dog like me?
Yes, yes, yes!

I am a bird, as GREEN as can be.
Is there room on the broom for a bird like me?
Yes, yes, yes!

I am a frog, as CLEAN as can be.
Is there room on the broom for a frog like me?
Yes, yes . . .
No!

I am a dragon, as MEAN as can be.
Is there room on the broom for a dragon like me?

NO, NO, NO!
OFF YOU GO!
Ho ho ho ho ho ho HO!

Have a singalong before or after your play!
Give a copy of the song lyrics to everyone in your audience
so they can read the words. Or why not turn your play into a
musical? You could act out the song instead of using the script for
a shorter performance. Or include the song as an extra part of
your performance – this is a good way of involving more children.

Performing with Large Groups

The Room on the Broom Play can be performed with smaller or larger groups of children, and even with an entire class.

Narrators and Winds

I've written the play with six narrators, but you can divide the role to have as many as you like, or only one. Similarly, you can have as many winds as you like, or combine them with the role of narrator.

Chorus

"And whoosh! they were gone" and "Iggety, ziggety, zaggety, ZOOM!" are lines that are fun for a chorus of children to say. (The audience can also join in! Practise with the audience before the play starts, so they know what to say.)

Stagehands

Some children can be stagehands, retrieving the witch's lost belongings and setting up chairs for the magnificent broomstick. They can also do sound effects, for example using wood blocks for the sound of the witch tapping the broomstick. The stagehands can wear black, with witches' or wizards' hats (see page 28 for instructions on how to make these).

Puppet Show
How about performing the play as a puppet show with finger puppets or sock puppets?

Notes for Staging the Play

The play can be performed on stage, in a classroom or at home, and the set can be as simple or as complicated as you would like.

Props

Broomstick: this could just be imaginary. Have the actors pretend to ride a broomstick, and then fall off when it breaks. If you want to make a real broomstick, you could use two pieces of hollow tube taped together in the middle which can be pulled apart when the broomstick breaks. This can be fiddly, so it would be a good idea to practise before your performance.

Cauldron: you can usually find these very easily in shops around Halloween, but you could use a black bucket with a handle instead.

Wand: try making a wand for the witch by cutting out a star from paper or cardboard and taping it to the end of a drinking straw or twig.

Costumes

The witch needs a cloak, hat (see page 28) and hair bow. You can make the bow out of cardboard and fix it to the witch's plait with Velcro – this will make it easy to take on and off during the performance. The witch also needs ginger hair worn in a plait – try looking online or in a fancy dress shop for a long ginger wig.

The animals and the dragon can wear face paints or simple homemade masks or headbands. You can also make a wind stick for Wind to wave by taping some long grey and white ribbons or strips of crêpe paper to a stick or hollow tube.

Make the Witch's Hat

Make a witch's hat for your play. Ask a grown-up for help.

You will need:
- 2 large sheets of black card
- sticky tape
- large dinner plate (to trace a circle)
- safety scissors
- pencil
- decorations

1. Roll one large sheet of black card into a pointed cone shape. Make sure the open end fits on your head. Stick the cone together loosely with sticky tape.

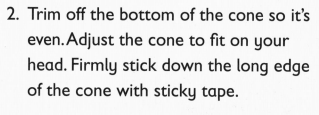

2. Trim off the bottom of the cone so it's even. Adjust the cone to fit on your head. Firmly stick down the long edge of the cone with sticky tape.

3. To make the brim of the hat, place the dinner plate onto the other sheet of black card and draw around it to make a circle. Cut out the circle.

4. Place the cone in the middle of the circle and draw around it to make another circle.

5. Draw a smaller circle about 2cm inside this one. Cut out the smaller circle.

6. Cut flaps from the inside circle to the pencil circle. Place the cone on the brim. Bend the flaps up inside the cone and stick down firmly with sticky tape.

7. Now decorate your witch's hat. If you're playing the witch in the play you will need ginger hair worn in a plait. If you don't have ginger hair, you could use a wig (you can find one online or at a fancy dress shop).

Activities

Posters and Programmes

Make posters to tell people when and where the play is happening. You could also make tickets for your audience and programmes to tell the audience who the actors and helpers are. A programme is a great souvenir for your audience.

To make a programme fold a piece of paper in half. Write the name of the play on the front and decorate it. Inside, write a list of the characters and who is playing them. Then add the names of everyone else who is helping with the play.

Design a Magnificent Broomstick

What would your magnificent broomstick be like? You could leave space on the back page of your programme for people to design their own magnificent broomsticks.

Witchy Snacks

Make these witchy snacks to share with your audience after the play. Ask a grown-up to help.

Cheesy Broomsticks

You will need:
- cheese slices
- pretzel sticks

Ask a grown-up to cut a cheese slice in half and make lots of small cuts along one edge. Roll the cheese around a pretzel stick and gently pull the strips apart to make your broom.

Chocolate Witches' Hats

You will need:
- chocolate
- ice cream cones
- chocolate biscuits
- decorations

Ask a grown-up to melt some chocolate. Carefully spread the melted chocolate on the outside of the ice cream cones. Use some melted chocolate to stick the cones to the biscuits. Now decorate your chocolate witches' hats!

Quick Tips

⭐ Remember that practice makes perfect. Rehearse before your big performance.

⭐ Practise your lines and ask someone to test you as you learn them.

⭐ Knowing who speaks before you and listening to what they say is called a cue. It's very important to know when you should speak, so try to learn your cues.

⭐ At the end of the play, remember to have the cast and crew take a big bow when the audience is clapping!